The Lost Giant

AND OTHER AMERICAN INDIAN TALES RETOLD

PICTURES
by
Violet Moore Higgins

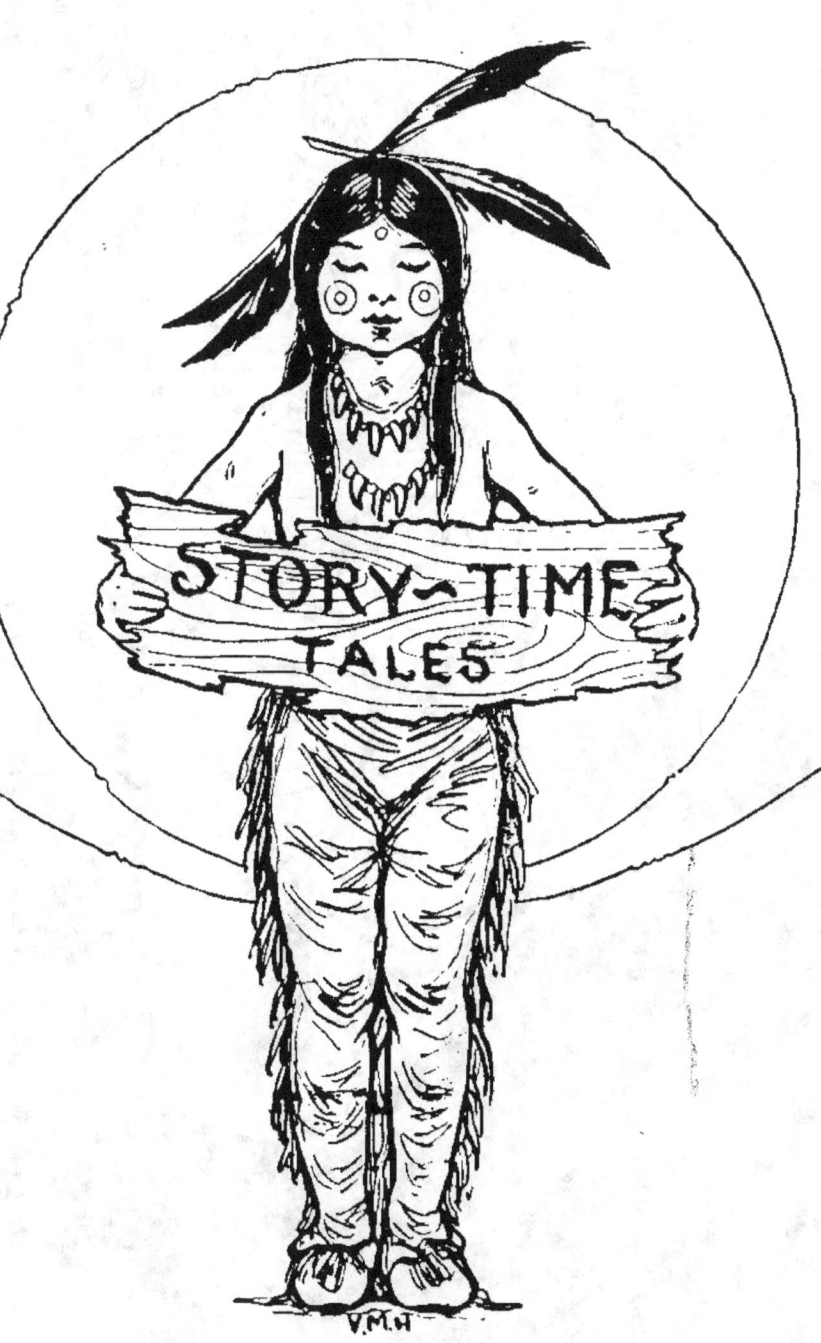

STORY~TIME TALES

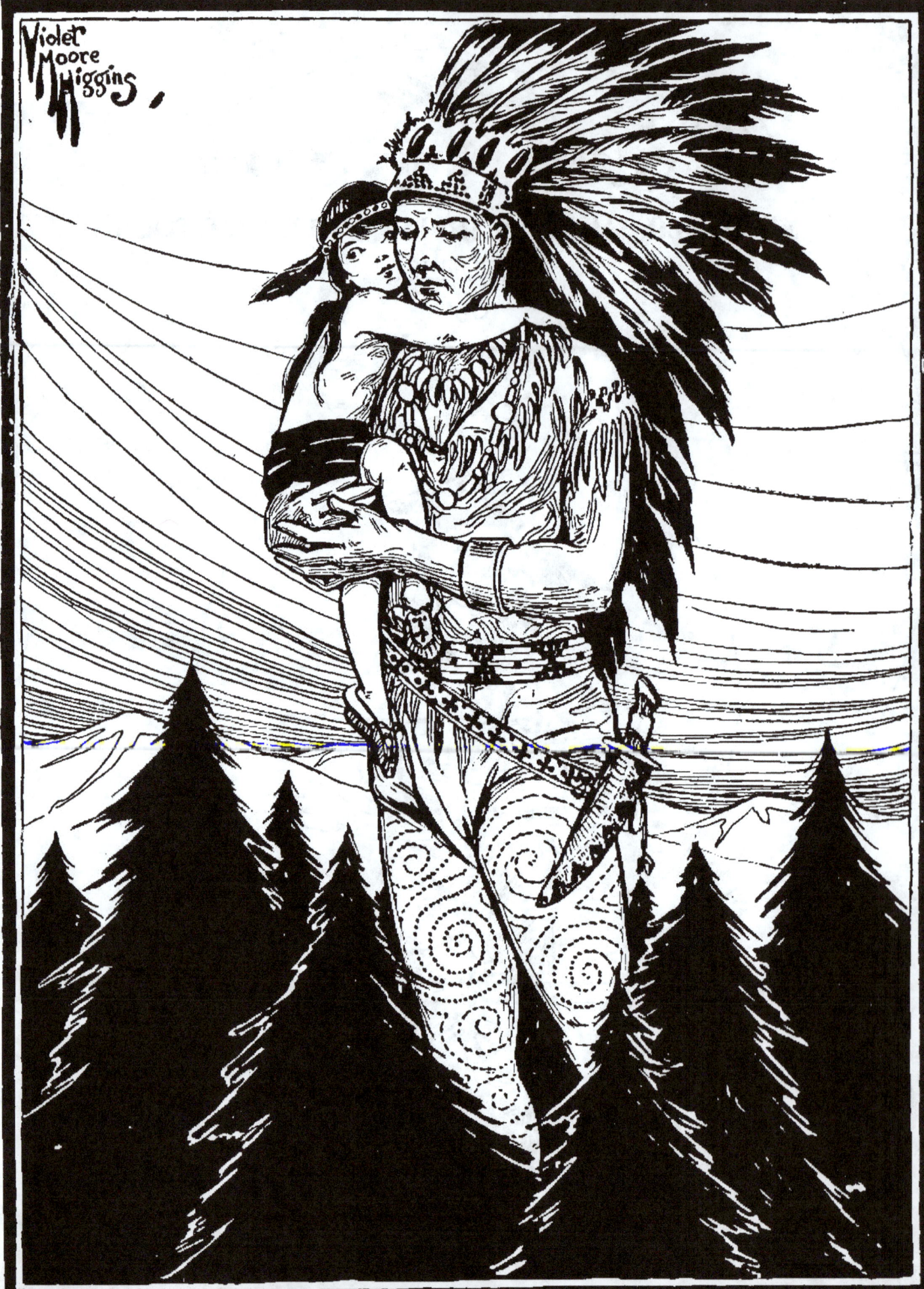

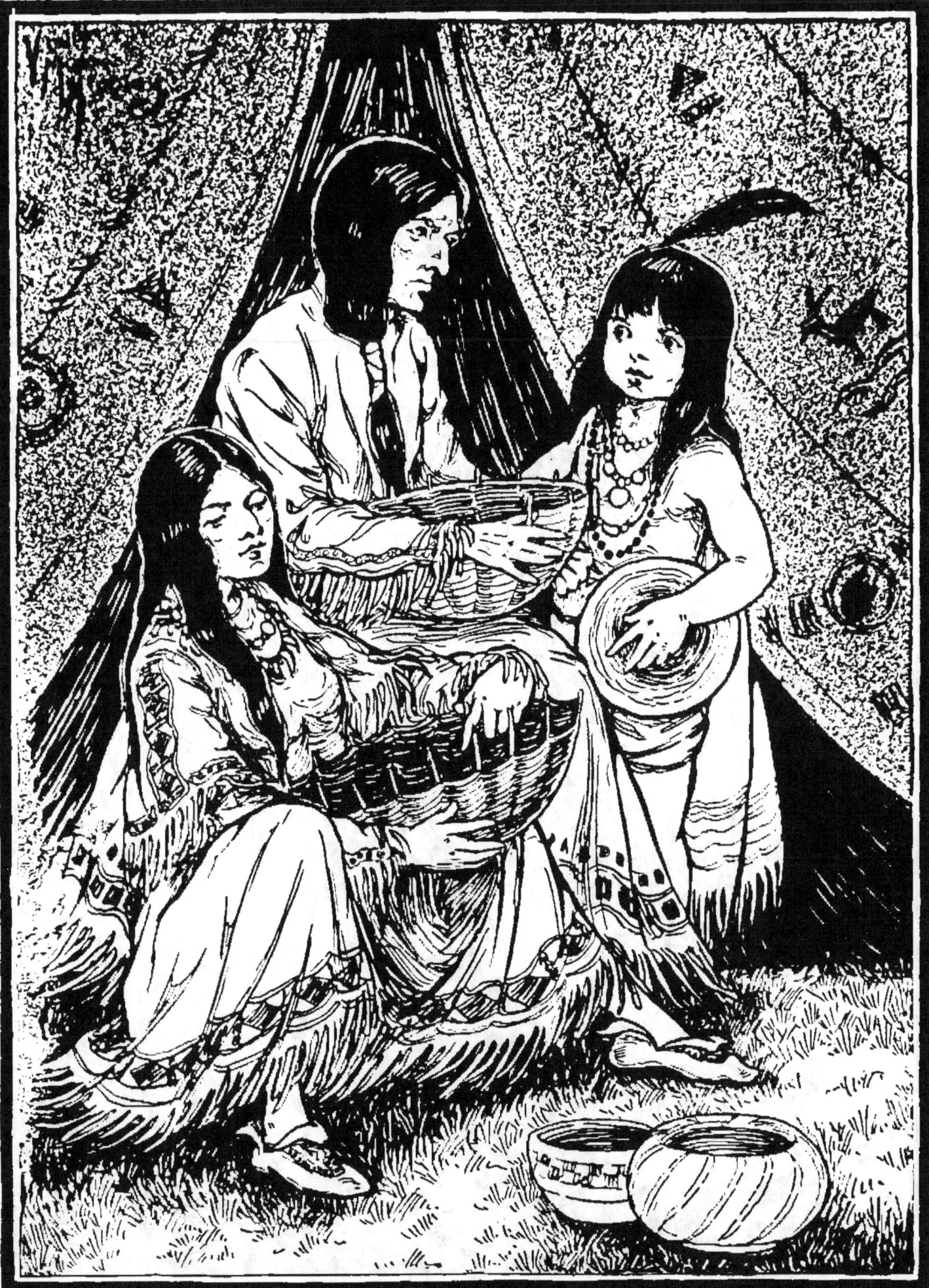

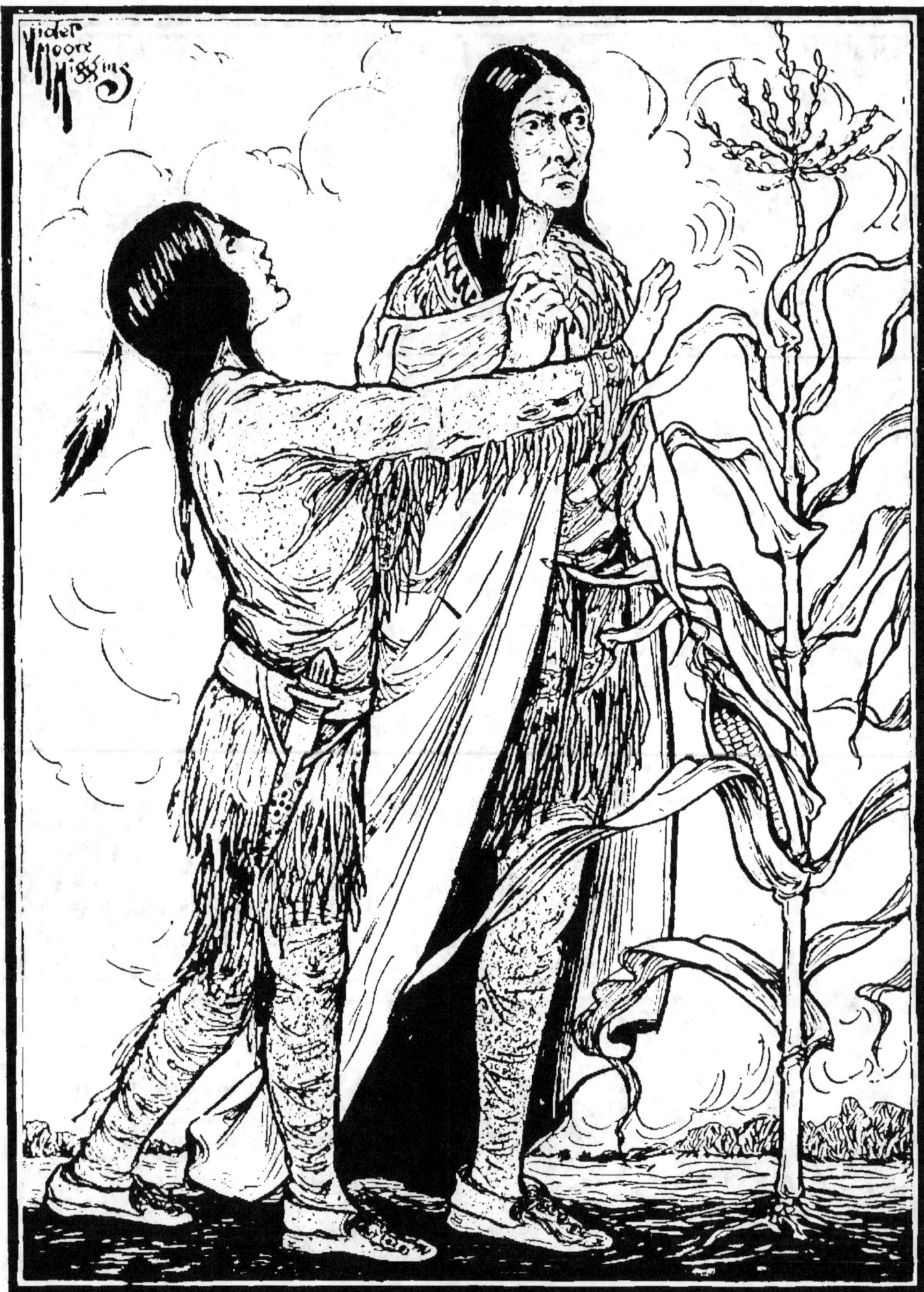

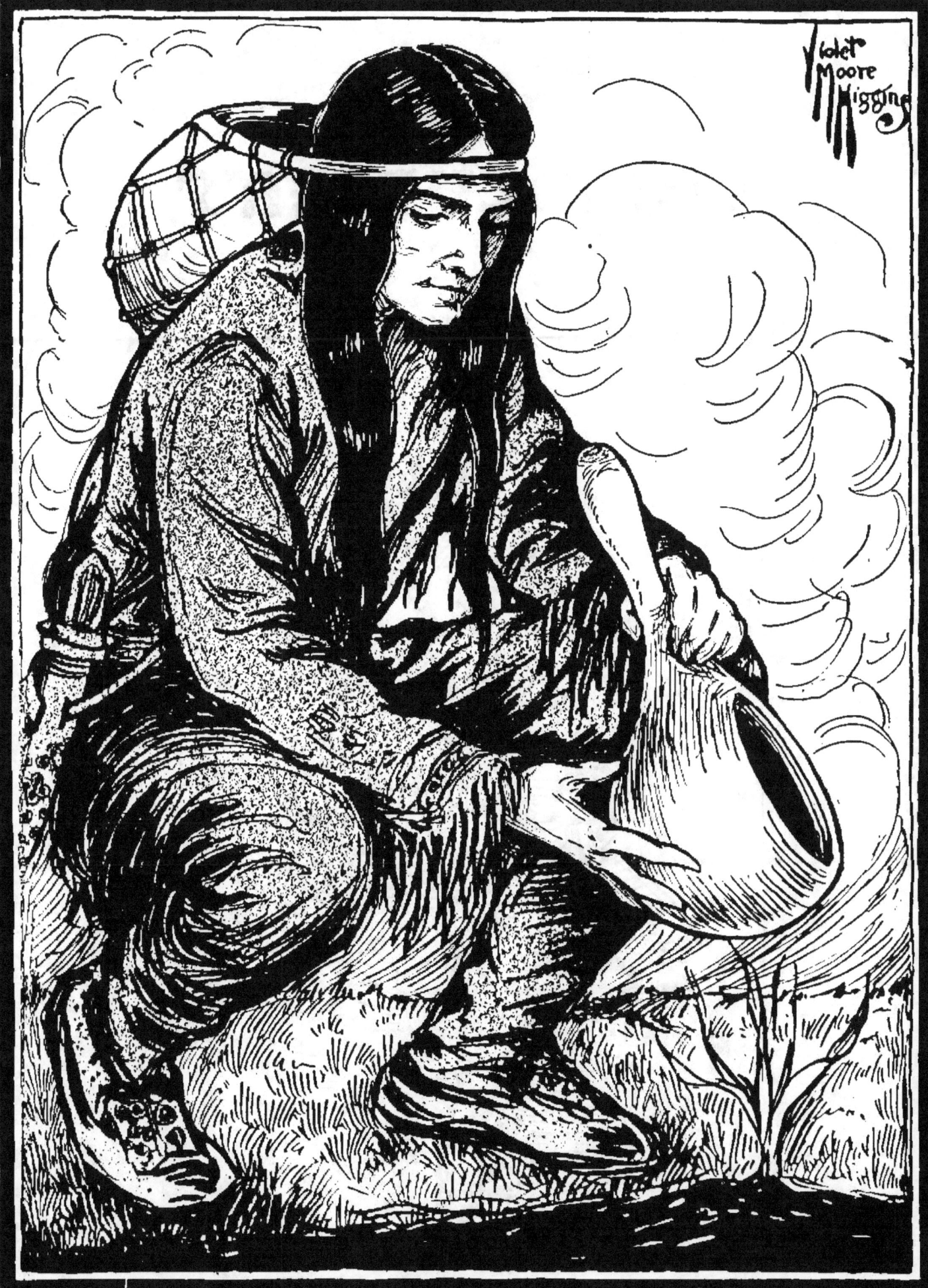

THE WOODCUTTER'S SON

And Other English Tales Retold

PICTURES BY
VIOLET MOORE HIGGINS

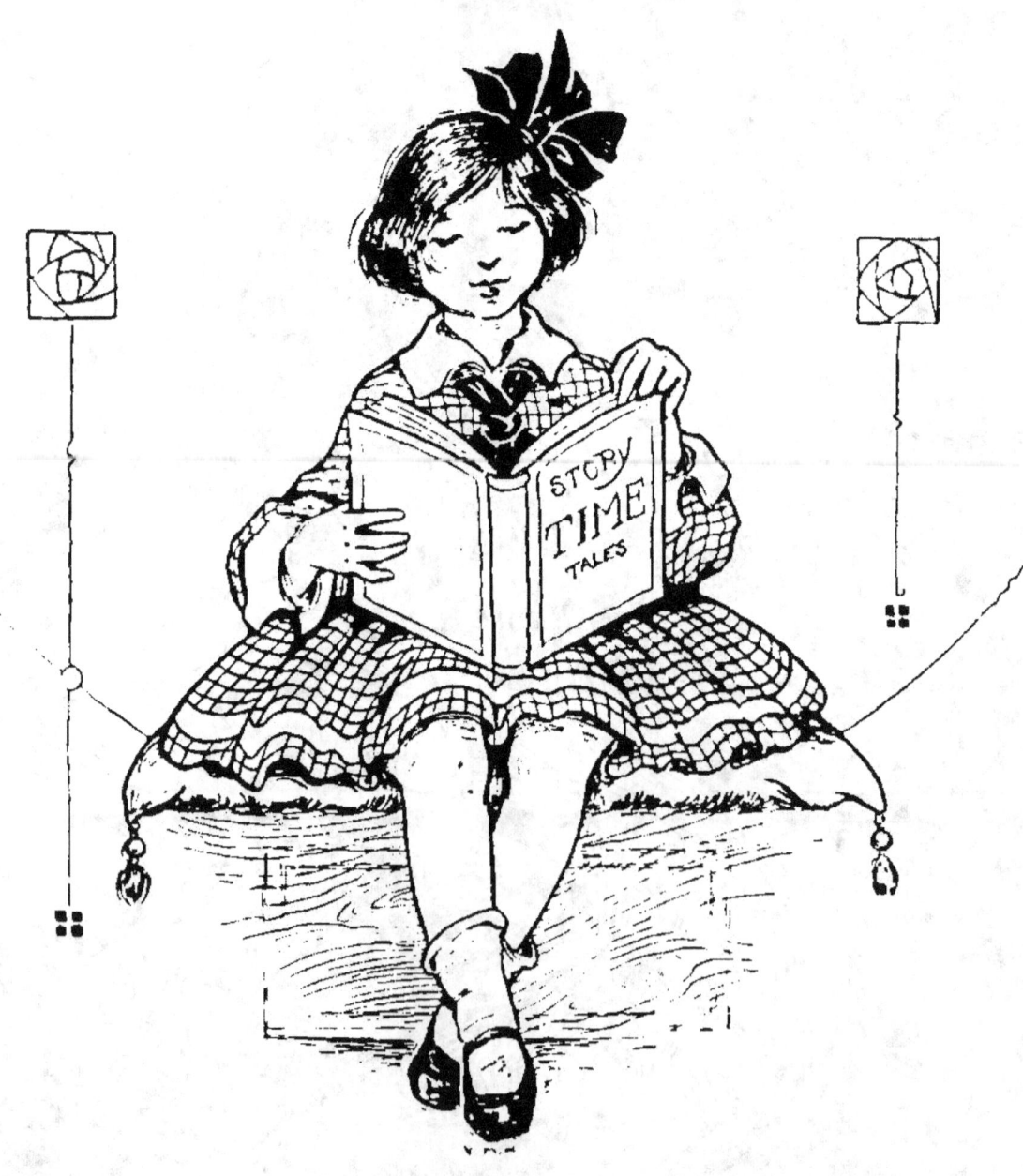

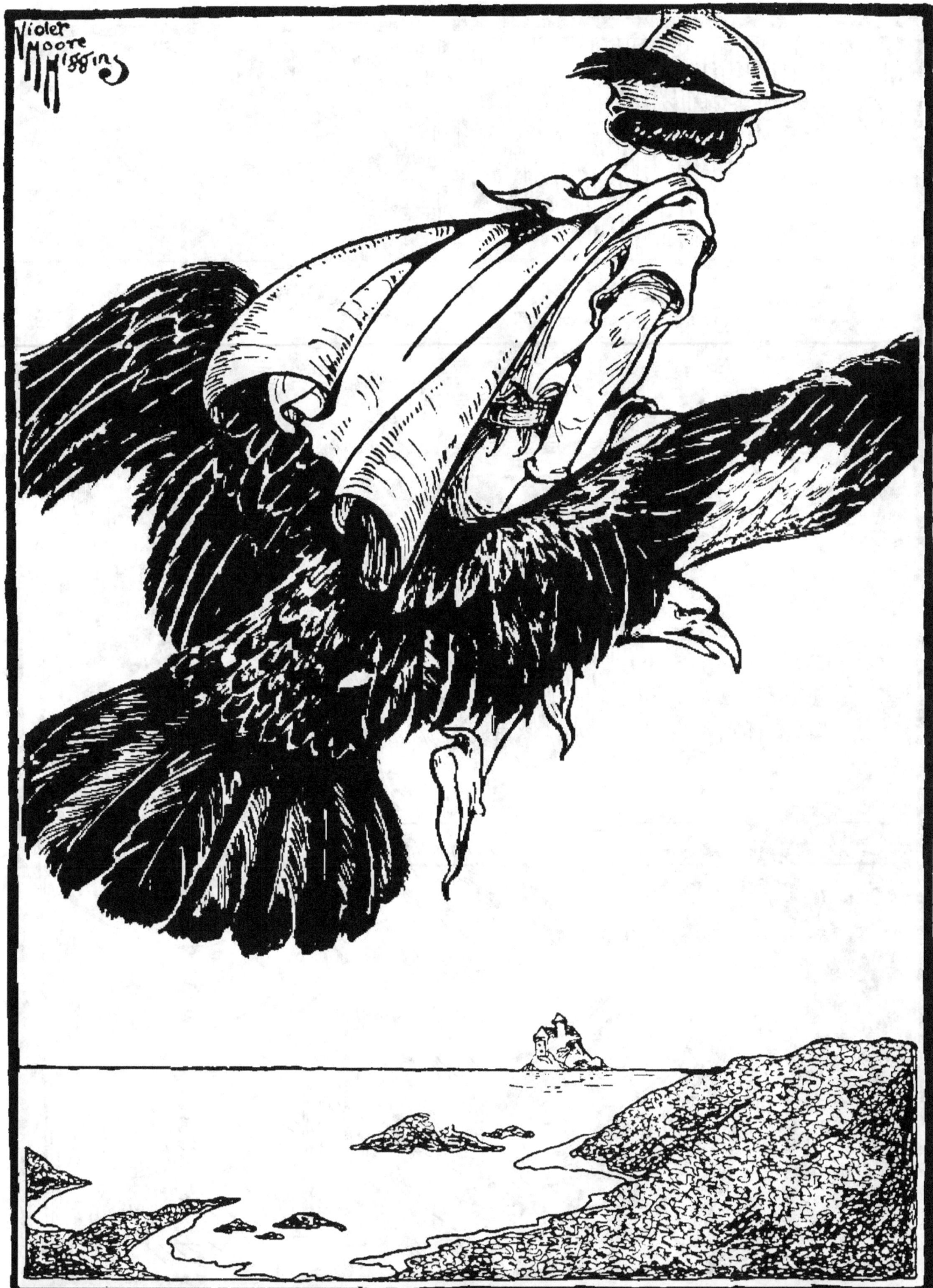

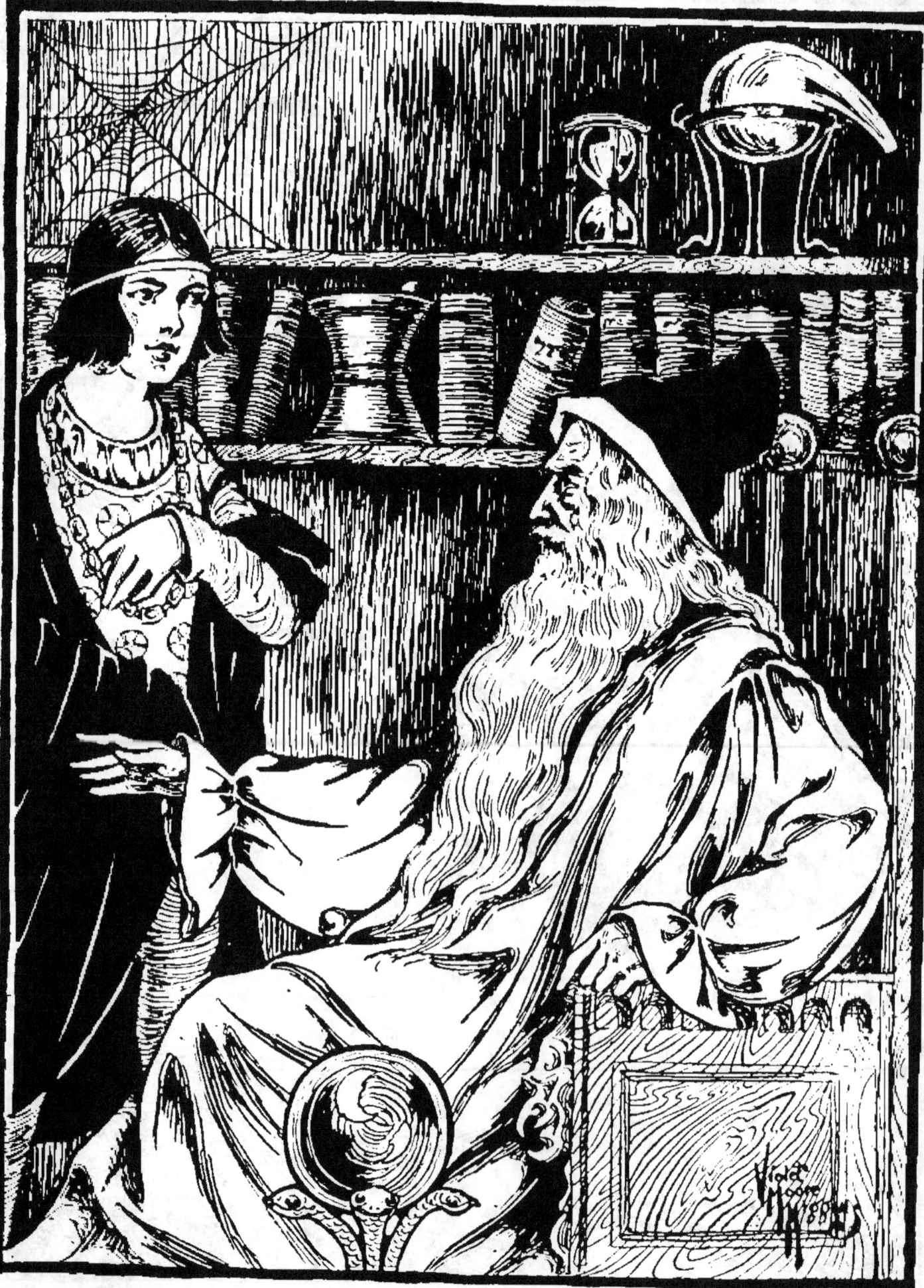

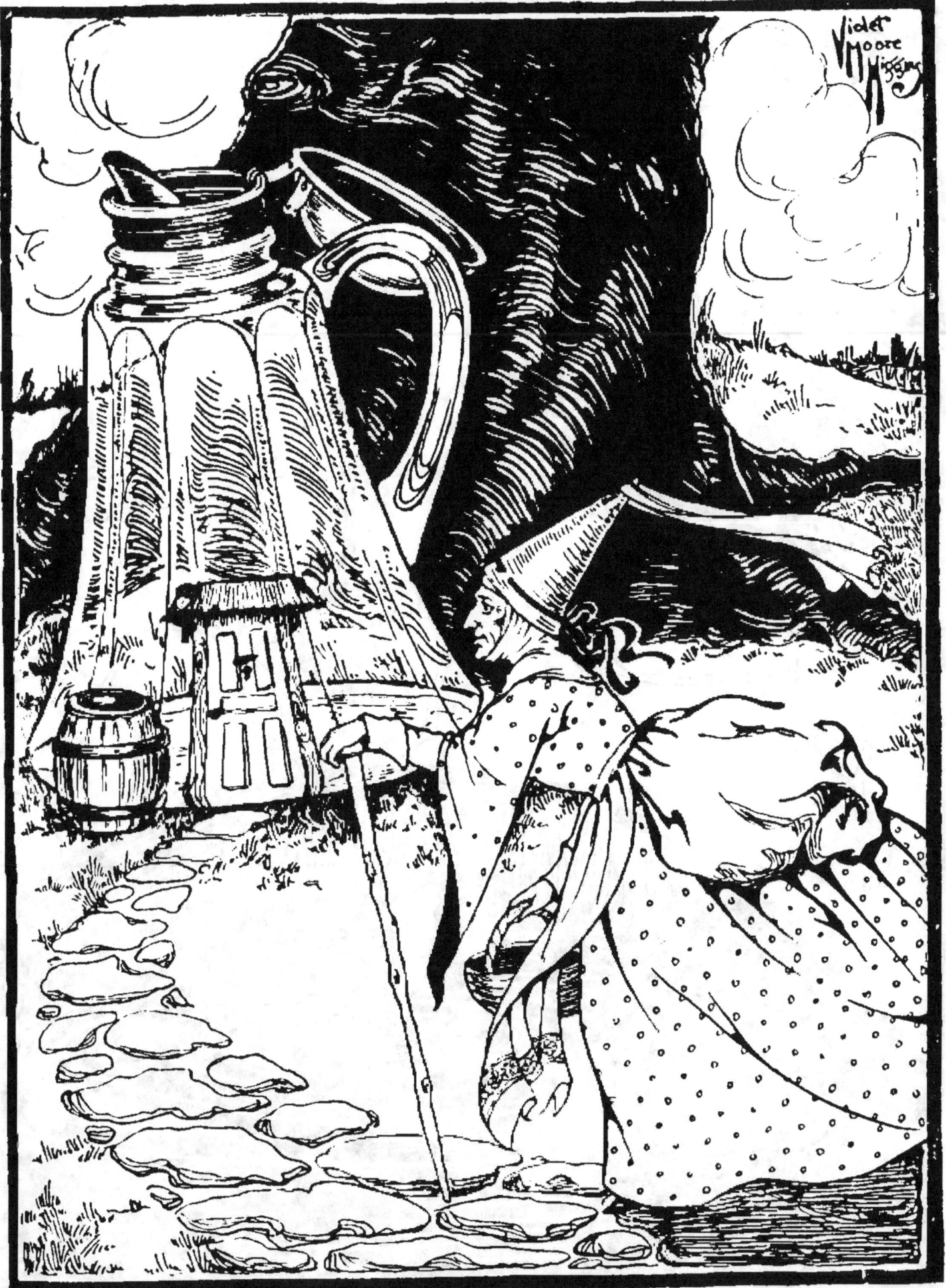

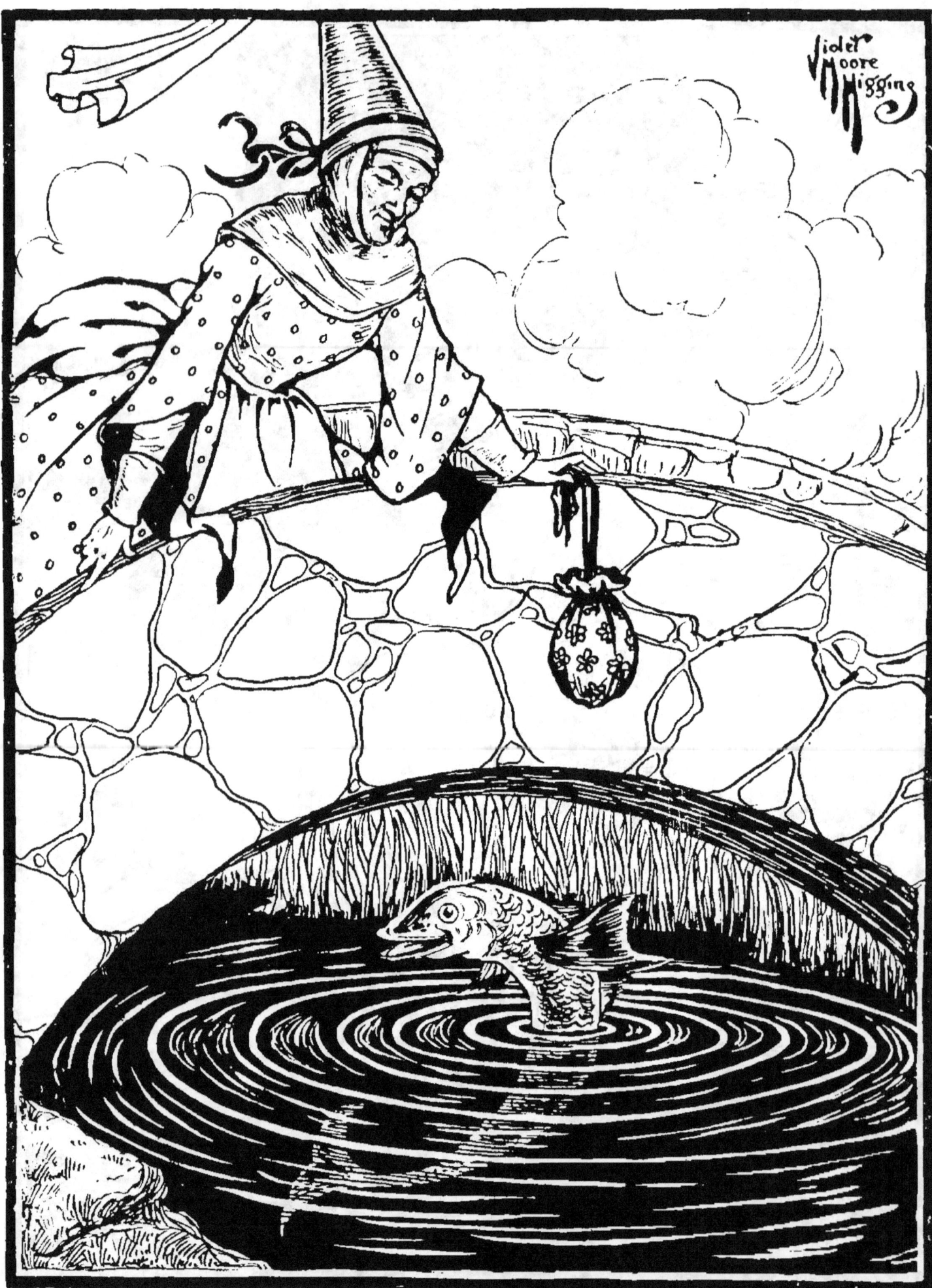

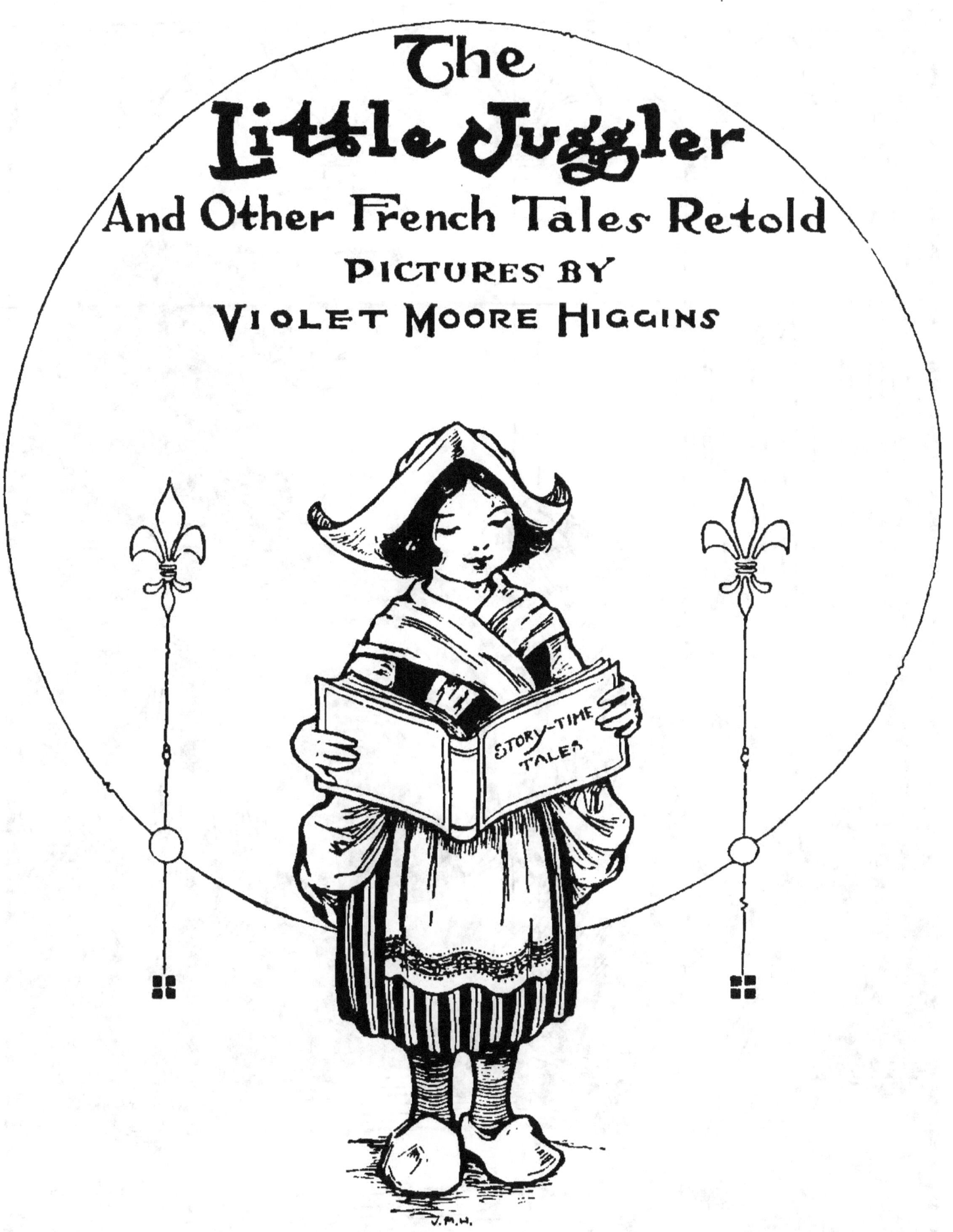

The Little Juggler
And Other French Tales Retold
PICTURES BY
VIOLET MOORE HIGGINS

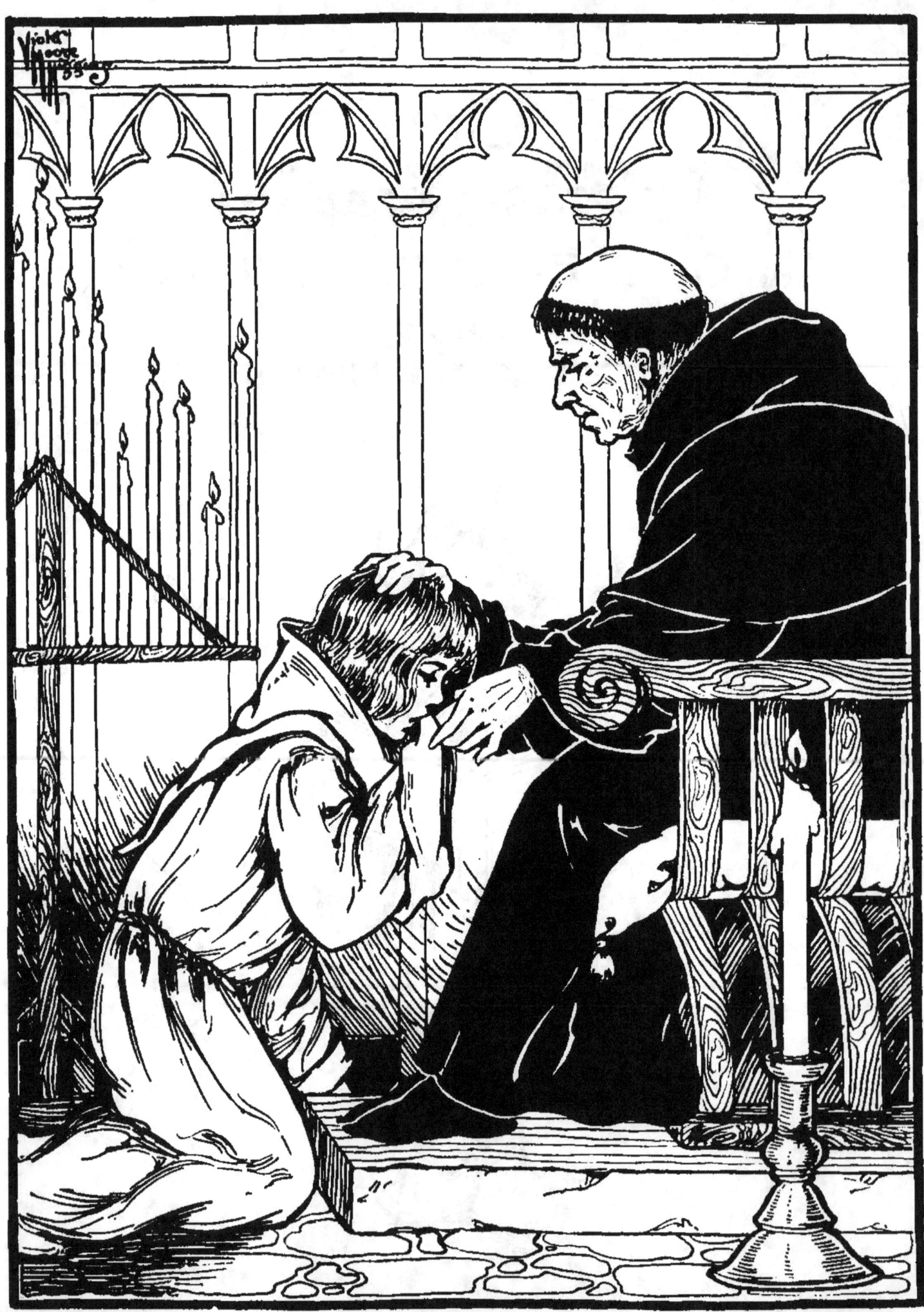

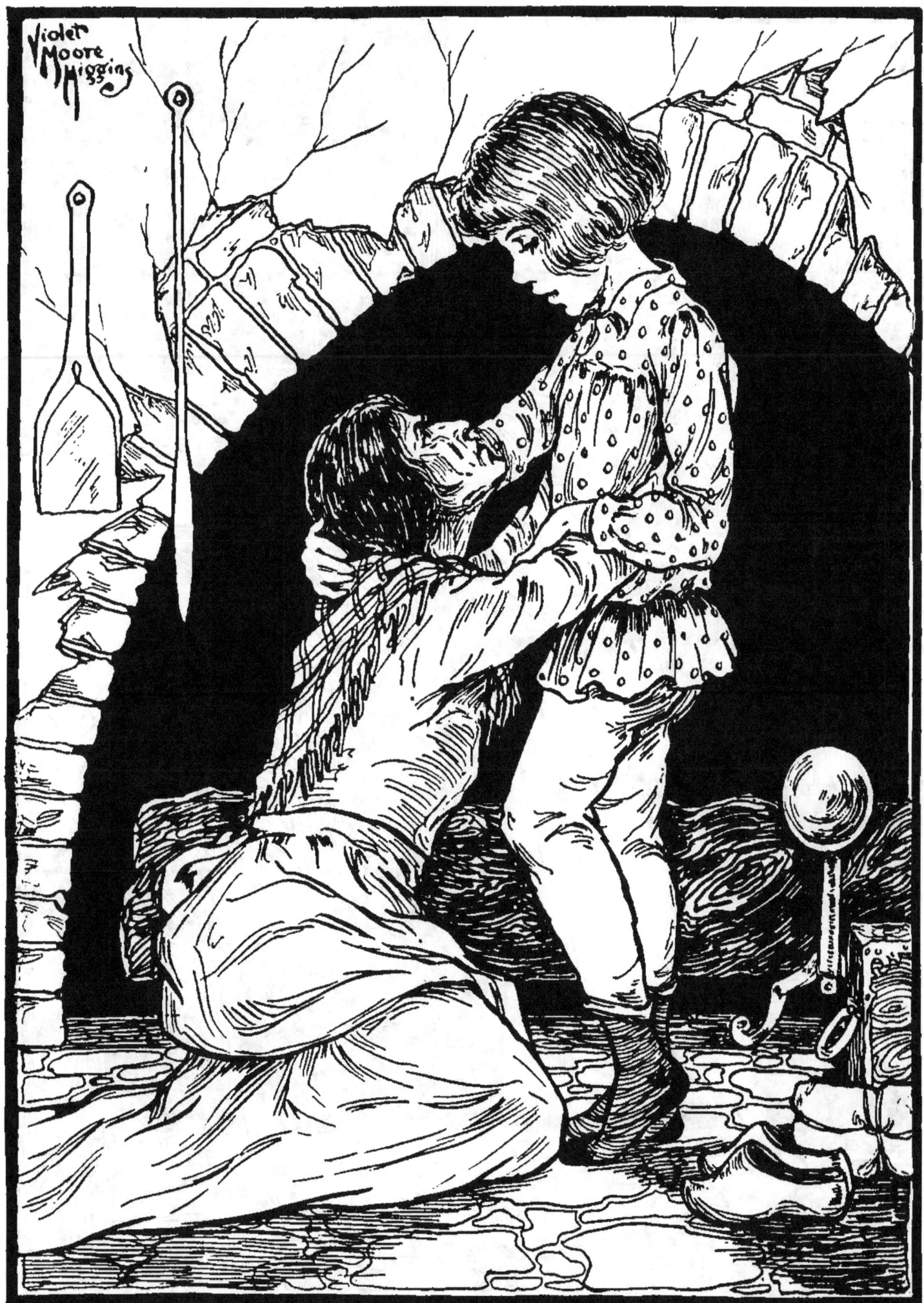

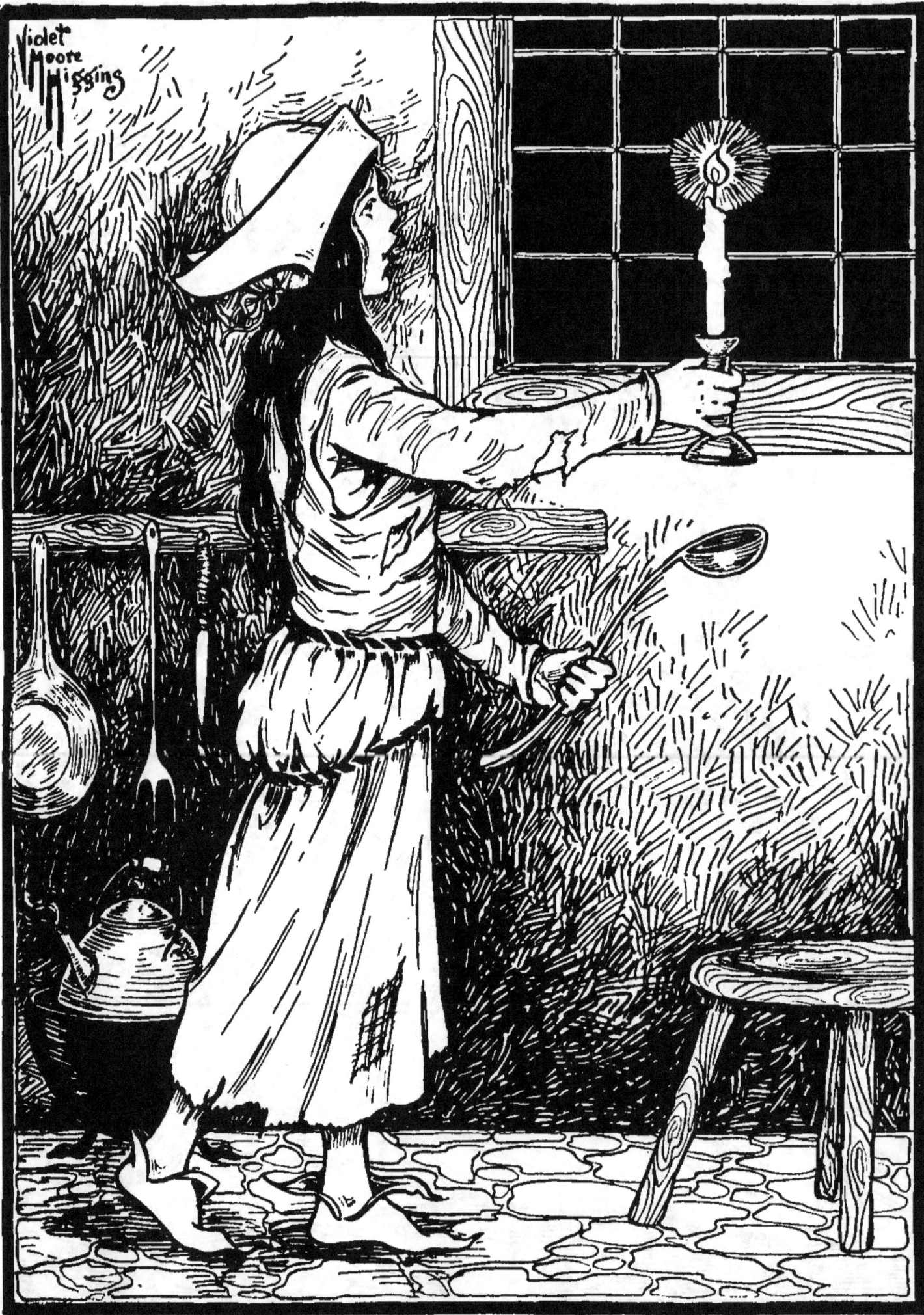

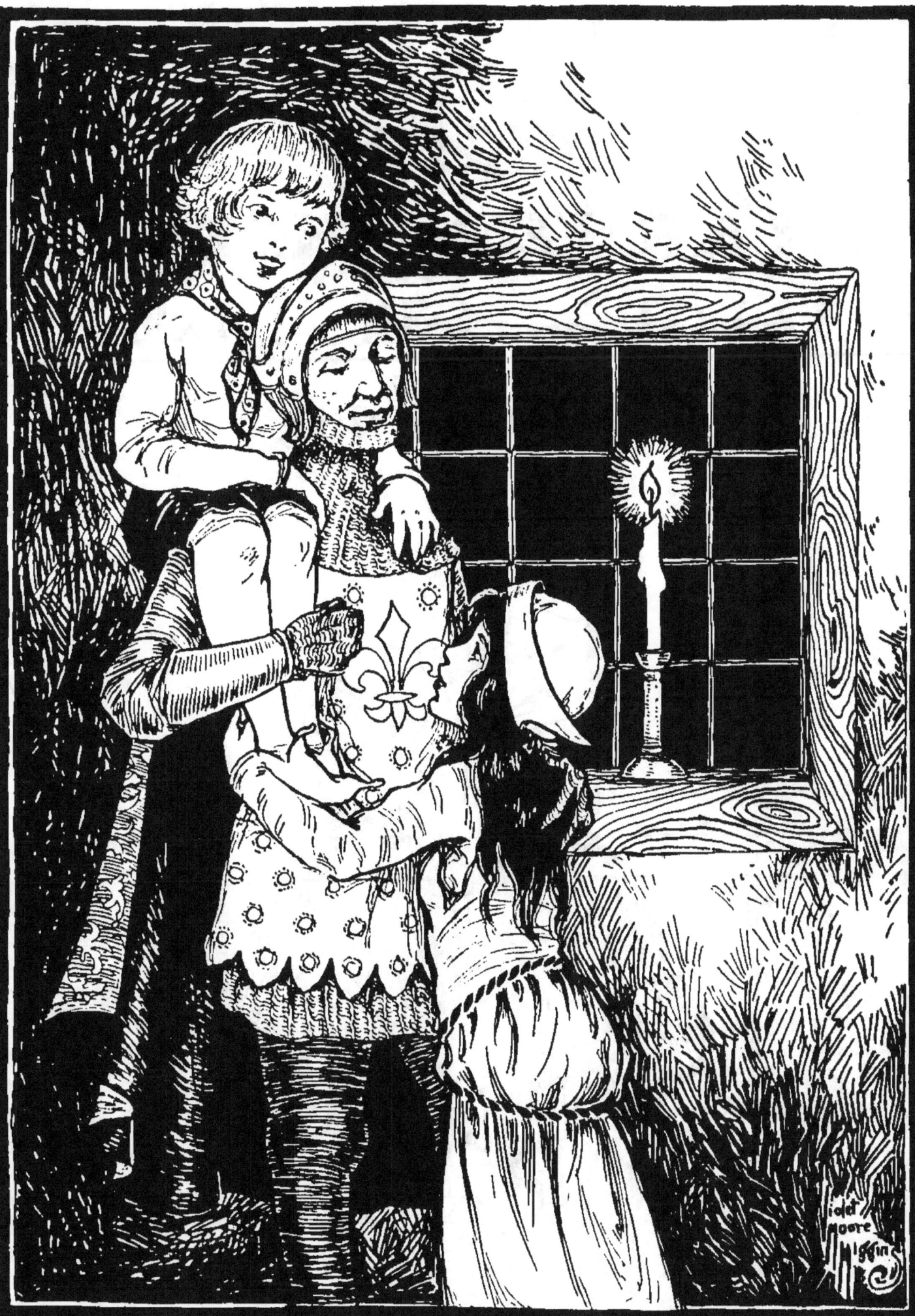

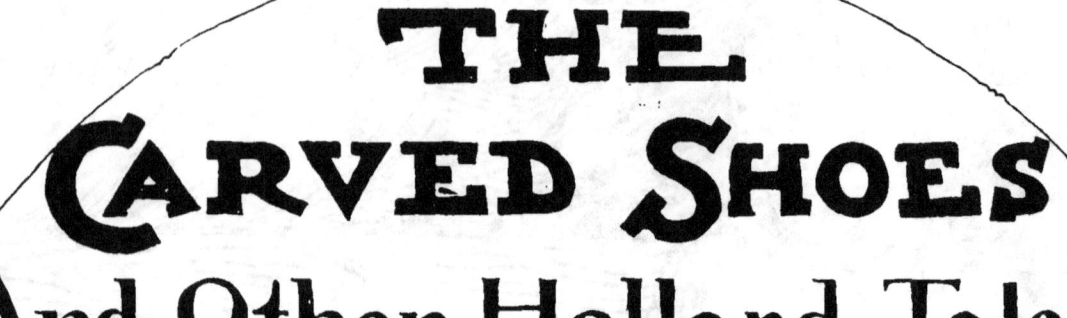

THE CARVED SHOES
And Other Holland Tales

PICTURES BY

Violet Moore Higgins

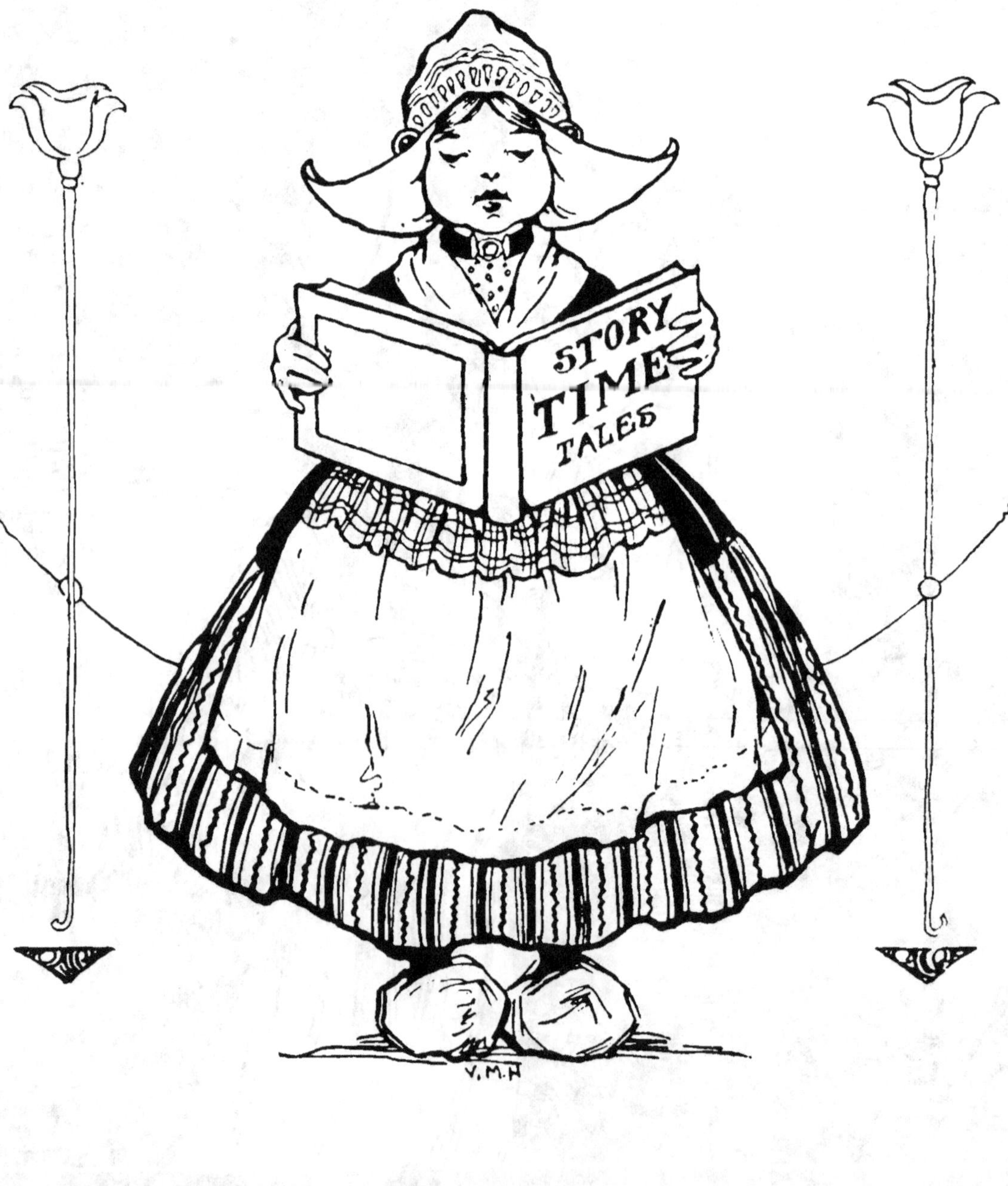

V.M.H

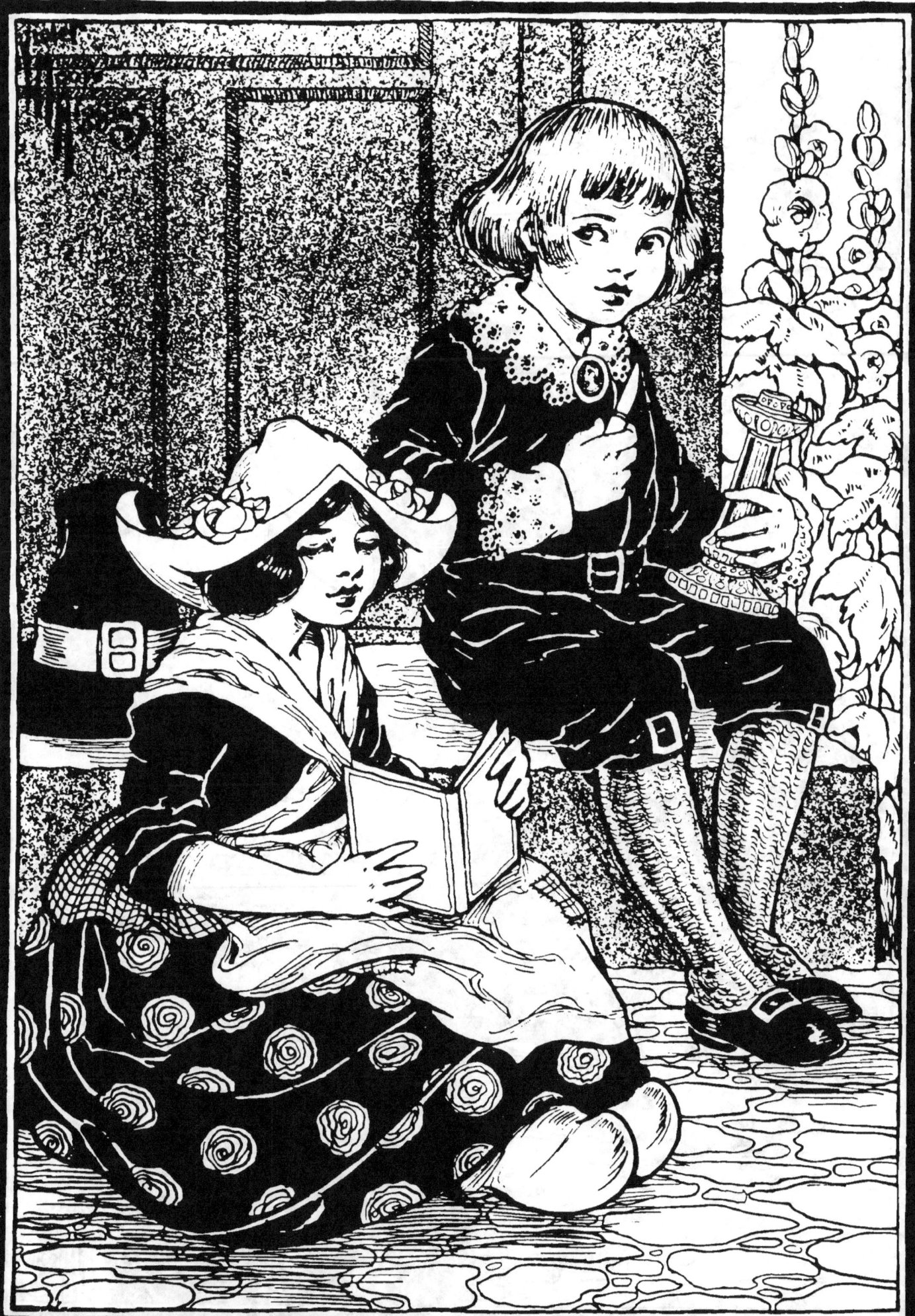

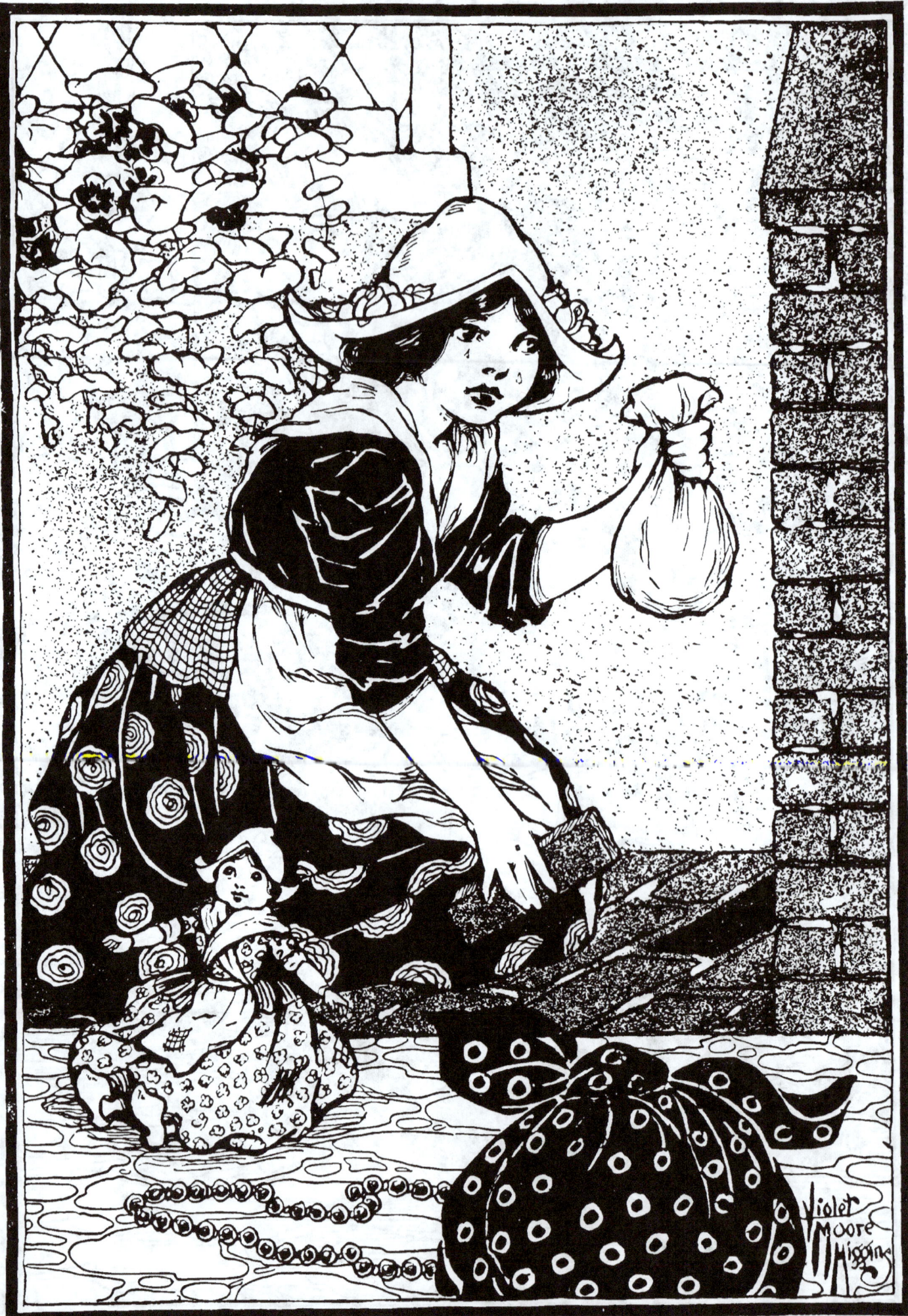

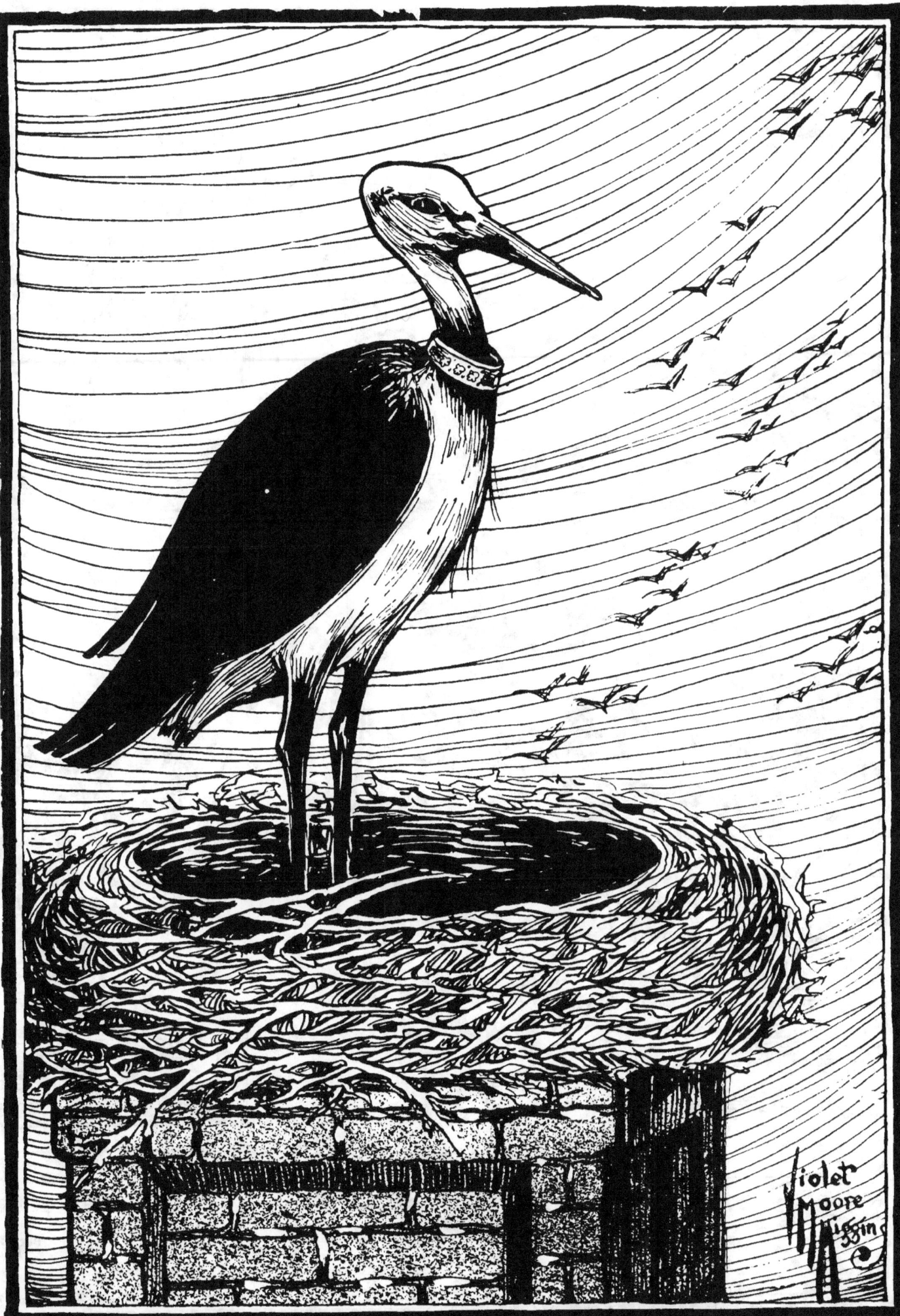

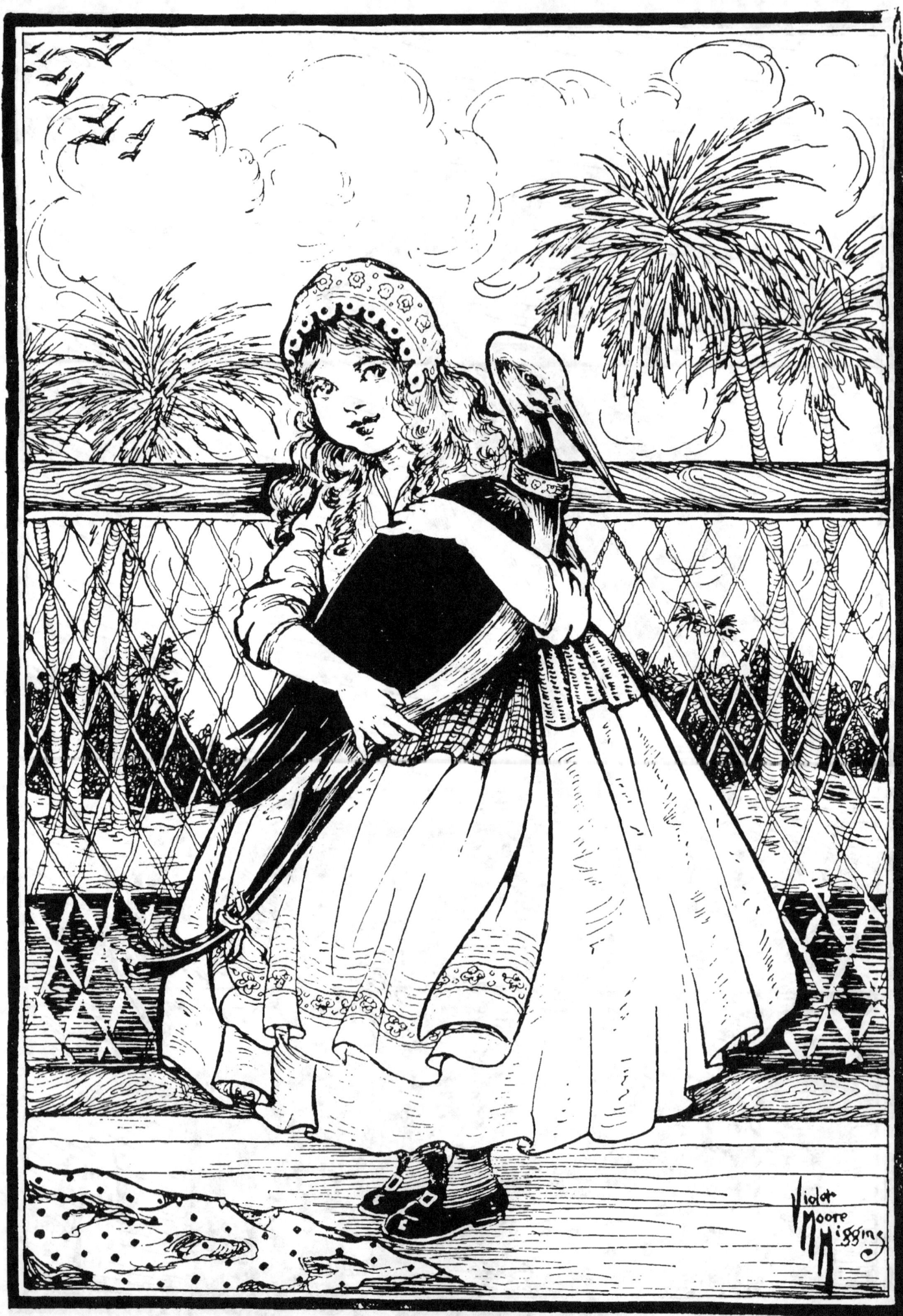

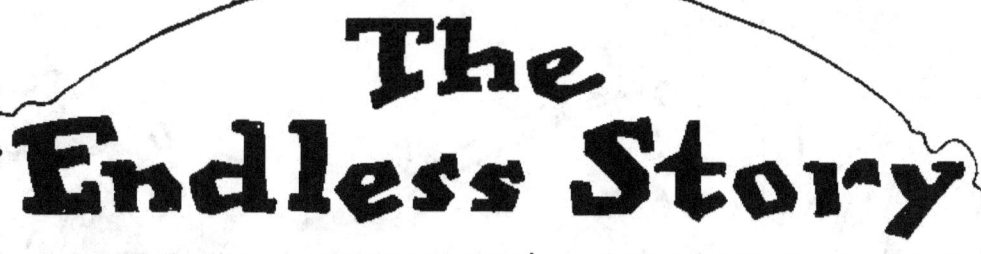

The Endless Story

AND OTHER ORIENTAL TALES RETOLD

PICTURES
by

Violet Moore Higgins

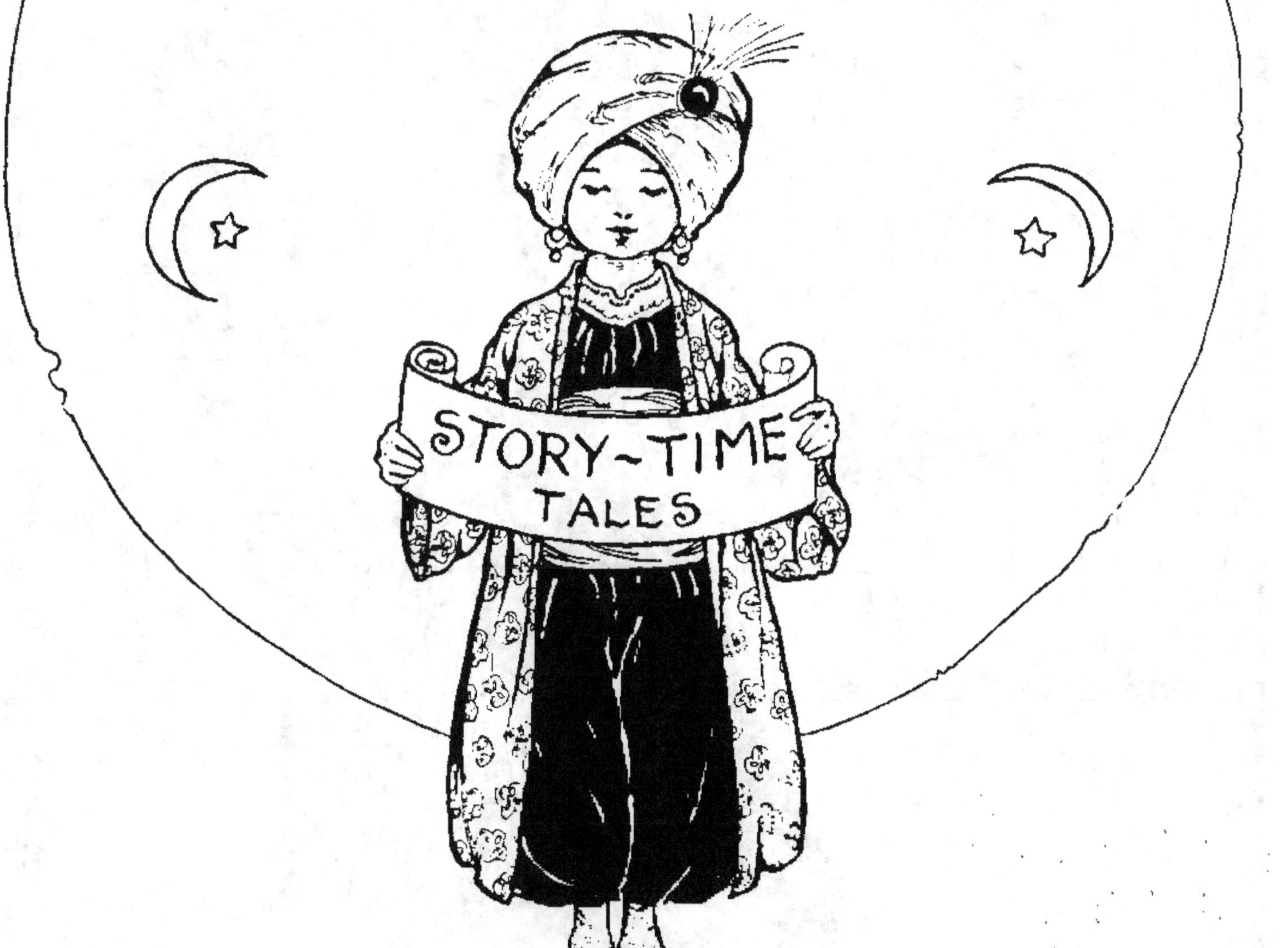

STORY~TIME
TALES

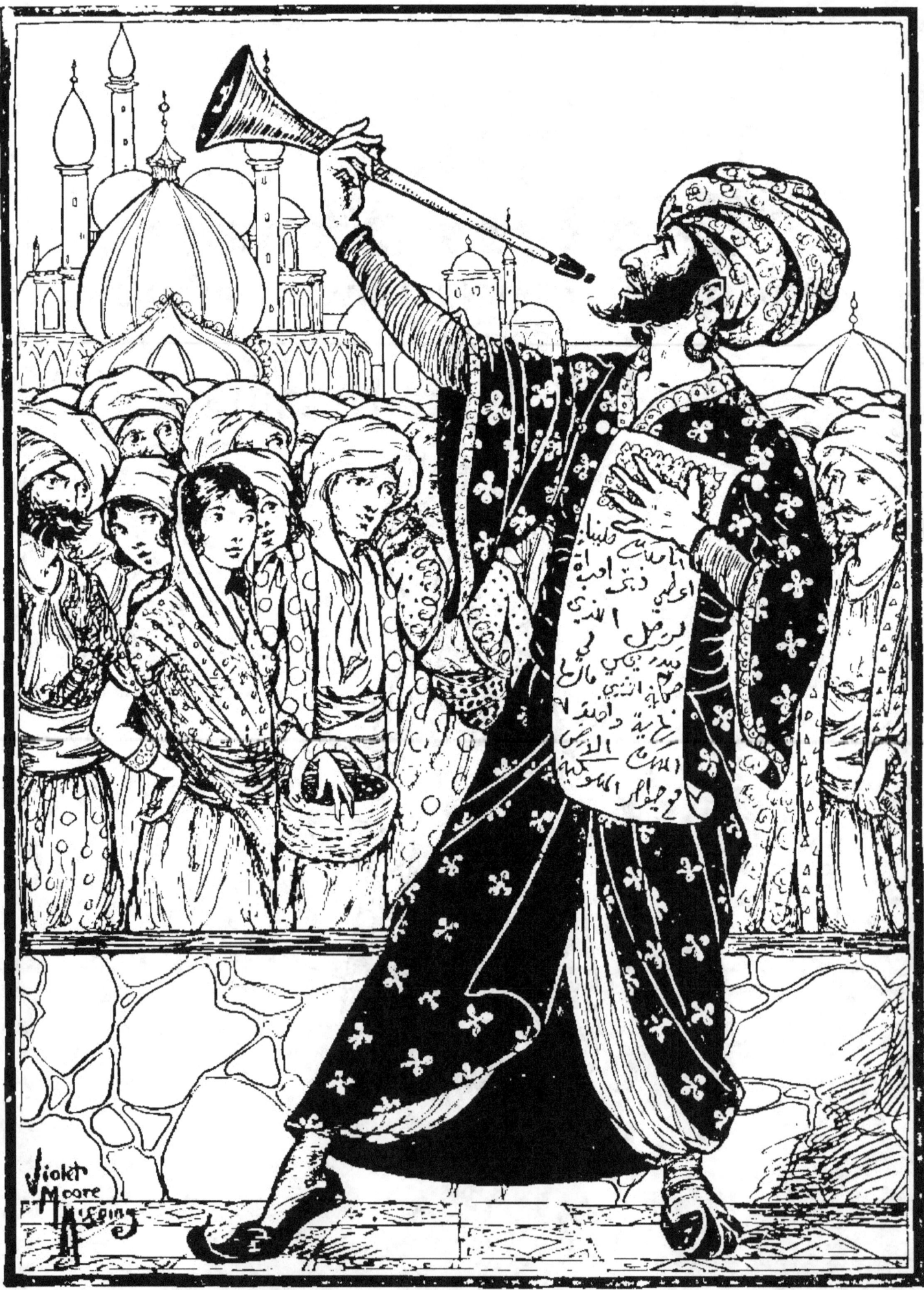

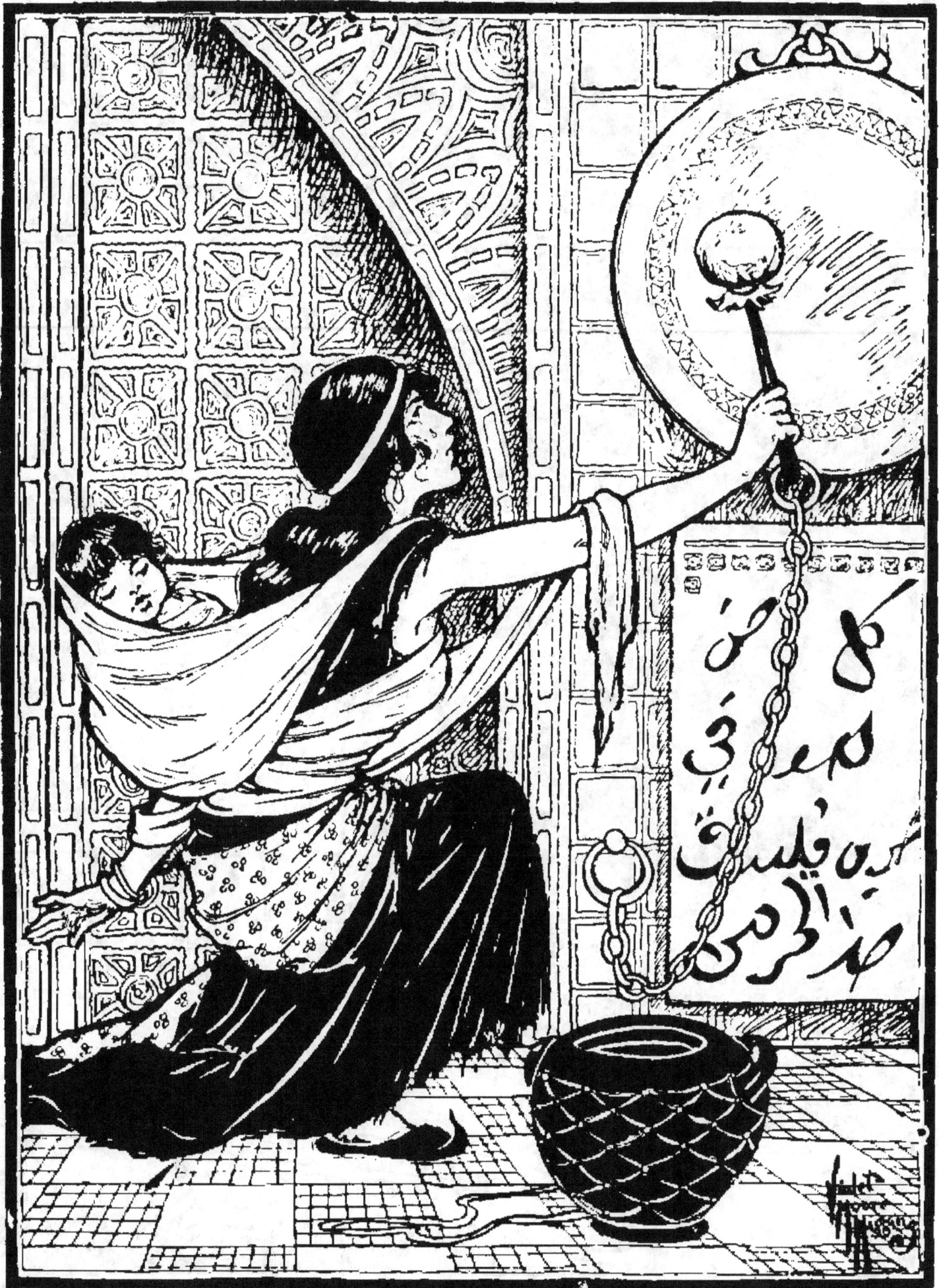

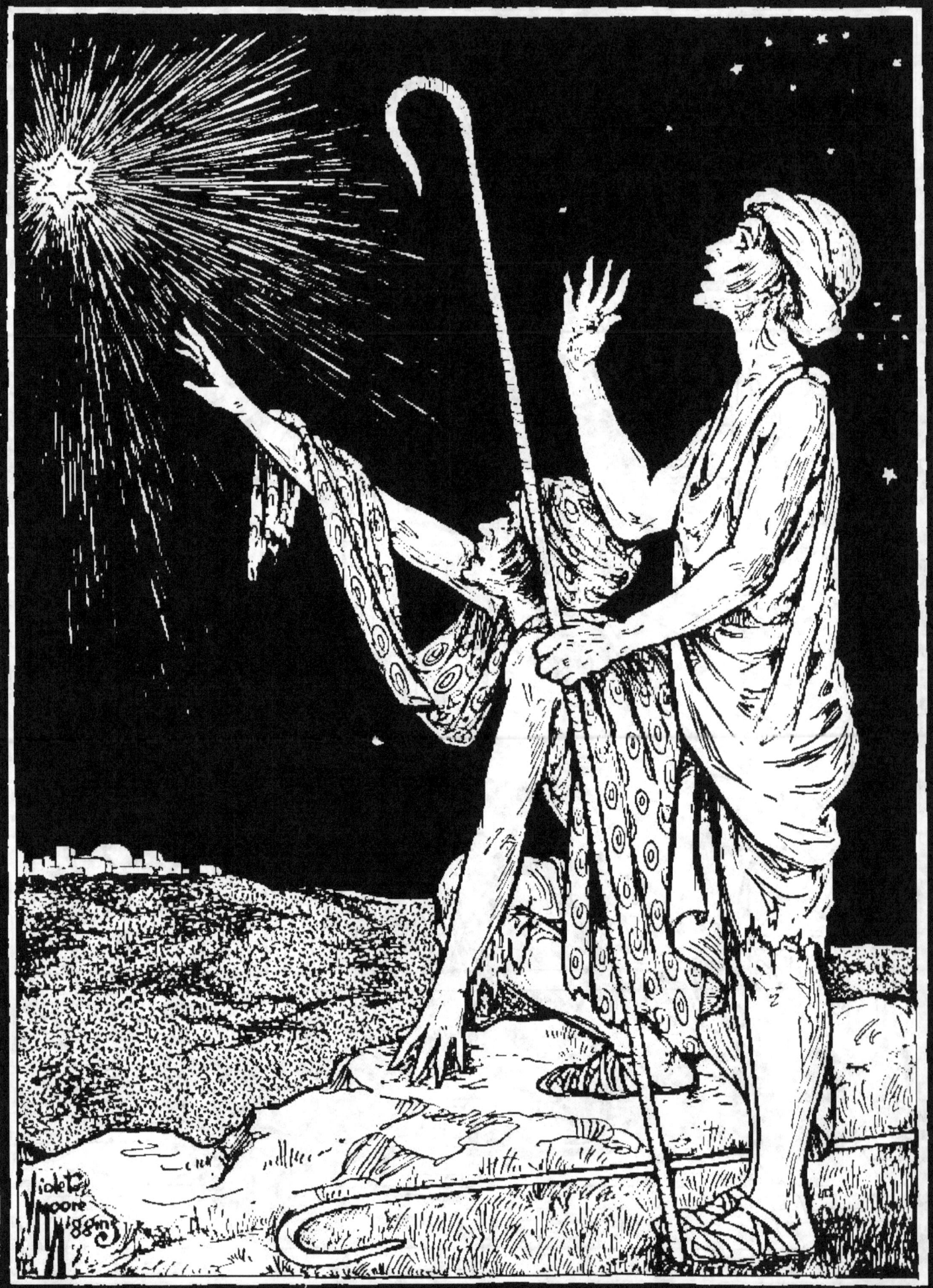

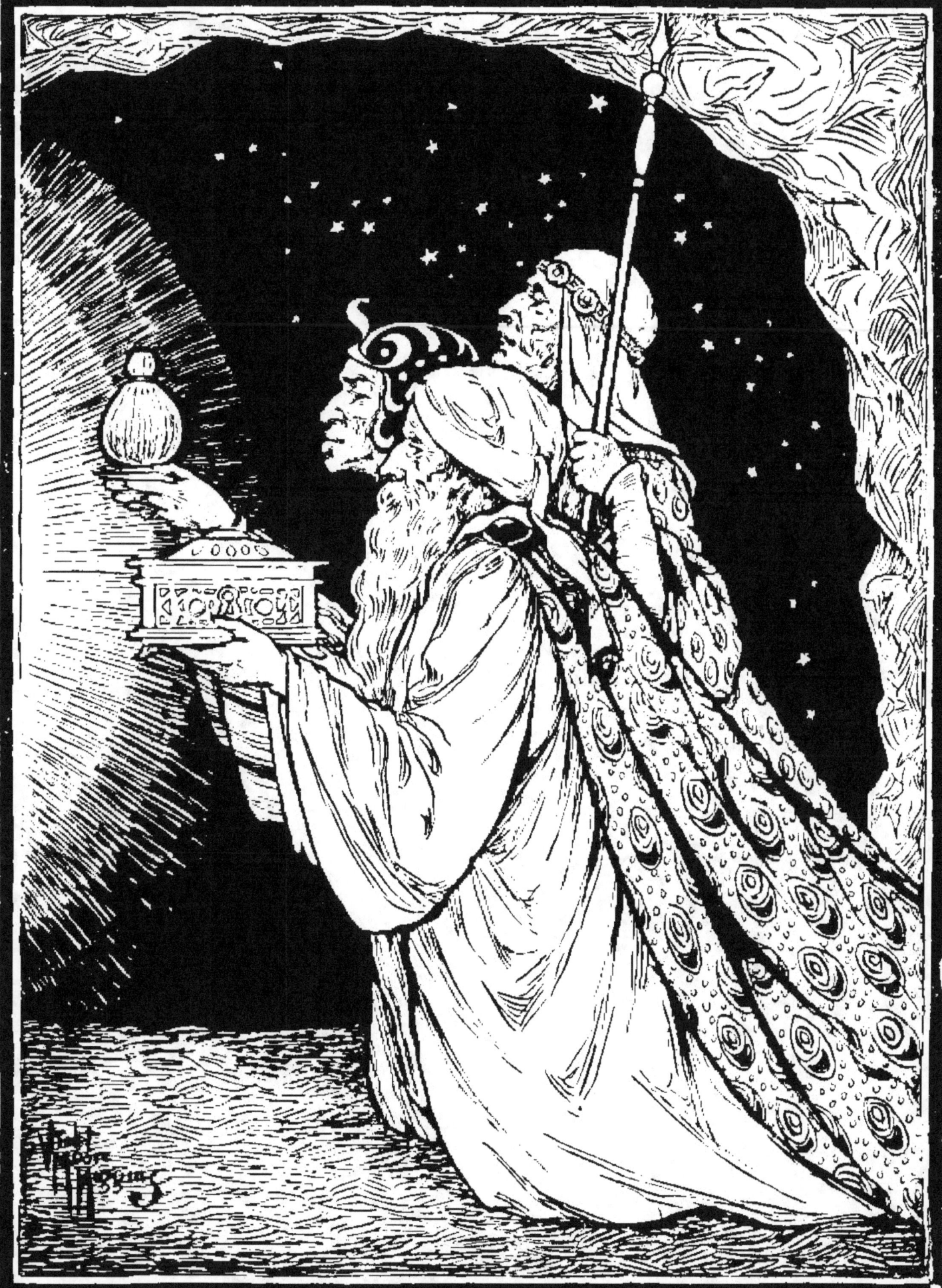